LET'S NAME
THE BABY

More than 3000 names and their meanings.

Key to abbreviations used in the following pages

Anglo-Saxon (AS)
Arabic (A)
Aramaean (Ar)
Celtic (C)
Danish (Da)
English (E)
French (F)
French-Celtic (FC)
French-Latin (FL)
Gaelic (Ga)
Greek (G)
Hebrew (H)
Hebrew-Latin (HL)
Italian (It)
Latin (L)
Middle English (ME)

Old English (OE)
Old French (OF)
Persian (P)
Sanskrit (San)
Saxon (Sa)
Scandinavian (Sc)
Slavonic (Sl)
Spanish (Sp)
Spanish-Arabic (SpA)
Spanish-Latin (SpL)
Swiss (Sw)
Teutonic (T)
Teutonic-Latin (TL)
Uncertain (U)
Welsh (W)

A

Aaron (H)	a mountain; tower of strength	Addison (AS)	Adam's descendant
Abbot (H)	father	Adelbert (T)	mentally brilliant
Abel (H)	breath	Adin (H)	sensual
Abelard (T)	resolute; ambitious	Adlai (H)	just
		Adolph (T)	noble hero
Abner (H)	paternal; bright	Adonis (G)	handsome
		Adrian (L)	pessimistic; man of the sea coast
Abraham (H)	tall; father of many		
Absolom (H)	peace loving	Ahab (H)	uncle
Achilles (G)	taciturn; sympathetic	Ahern (C) Ahearn	Lord of the horses
Adair (C)	from the oak-tree ford	Ainsley (OE)	of a nearby meadow
Adam (H)	man	Alan (C) Allan Allen Allyn	cheerful; in harmony
		Alaric (T)	ruler of all
		Alastair Allister (G) Alaster	see Alexander
		Alban (L) Albin	white
		Albert (T)	firm; responsible; noble
		Alcott (C)	from the stone cottage
		Alden (OE)	old friend

Aldous (T)	old; wise	**Archibald** (T)	holy prince;
Aldrich (T)	king	**Archie**	extremely bold
Alexander (G)	leader; defend-	**Arden** (L)	eager; sincere
Alex	er of men	**Armand** (F)	public
Alec			spirited
Alfred (OE)	of good coun-	**Armstrong** (OE)	with a
	sel; kingly		strong arm
Alger (AS)	spearman	**Arne** (Sc)	eagle

Aldous (T) — old; wise
Aldrich (T) — king
Alexander (G) / Alex / Alec — leader; defender of men
Alfred (OE) — of good counsel; kingly

Alger (AS) — spearman
Algernon (F) — prosperous
Alison (T) — of holy fame
Alonzo (G) — ready; willing
Aloysius (L) — Grace
Alphonse (T) — ready for battle

Alston (OE) / Alton — from the old manor or village
Alva (H) — tall
Alvin (T) — noble friend; beloved of all

Ambrose (G) — immortal
Amery (T) / Amory — industrious
Amos (H) — strong; courageous
Anatole (G) — of the East
Andrew (G) / Andre / Andy — manly
Angelo (G) — angel; messenger

Angus (C) — exceptional
Anselm (T) — divine helmet of God

Anson (AS) — son of Ann
Anthony (L) / Antonio / Antony — incomparable; praiseworthy

Archibald (T) / Archie — holy prince; extremely bold
Arden (L) — eager; sincere
Armand (F) — public spirited
Armstrong (OE) — with a strong arm
Arne (Sc) — eagle

Arno (T)	eagle	**Ashley** (AS)	dweller in
Arnold (T)	strong as		the ash tree
	an eagle		meadow
Arthur (C)	high-minded;	**Aubrey** (T)	ruler of the elves
	strong as	**Auburn** (U)	fine-appearing
	a rock	**August** (L)	venerable
Arvid (Sc)	eagle forest	**Augustus** (L)	majestic;
Arvin (T)	friend of		imperial
	the people	**Austin** (L)	useful
Asa (H)	healer	**Averill** (AS)	of April
Asher (H)	fortunate	**Axel** (H)	man of peace

Bailey (OF)	Bailiff or	**Baruch** (H)	blessed
Baylen	steward	**Basil** (G)	royal
Baird (C)	bard or	**Bayard** (F)	of fiery hair
	minstrel	**Baxter** (OE)	baker
Baldwin (T)	friendly; bold	**Benedict** (L)	blessed
Bancroft (AS)	from the	**Benjamin** (H)	
	bean field	**Ben**	son of the
Barclay	see Berkeley	**Bennie**	right hand;
Barlow (OE)	dweller on the	**Benny**	surety
	bare hill	**Bennett**	see Benedict
Barnet	see Bernard	**Benton** (AS)	of the moors
Barnaby (H)	son of	**Berkeley** (AS)	from the
	consolation		birch meadow
Barrett (T)	'bear-like	**Bernard** (T)	
Barrie (C)	straight-	**Bernhard**	bold as a bear
Barry	forward	**Bernie**	
Bartholomew		**Bert** (T)	
Bart (H)	warlike son	**Bertram**	bright

Beverley (AS)	from the beaver meadow	**Brand** (U)	a fighter
		Brant (T)	firebrand
Bevan (C)	} son of Evan	**Brent** (OE)	from the steep hill
Bevin			
Bill		**Brett** (C)	a Breton
Billie	} see William	**Brian** (C)	strong; sincere
Billy			
Blaine (C)	thin or lean	**Brice** (C)	ambitious
Blair (C)	a place	**Brigham** (OE)	dweller by the bridge
Bob	} see Robert		
Bobby		**Bromley** (OE)	dweller in the meadow
Booth (T)	home lover		
Borden (OE)	he lives near the boar's den	**Brock** (C)	badger
		Bruce (Ga)	positive; daring
Boris (SL)	warrior	**Bruno** (T)	brown
Bowen (C)	son of Owen	**Bryan**	} see Brian
Boyd (C)	yellow-haired	**Bryant**	
Bradford (AS)	from the broad ford	**Bryce** (C)	ambitious
		Burgess (T)	a townsman
Bradley (AS)	from the broad meadow	**Burke** (T)	from the castle
		Burton (AS)	of bright fame
Bramwell (OE)	of Abraham's well	**Byron** (T)	from the cottage

Cadwallader (Sc)	valiant in war	**Caleb** (H)	a dog lover
Cadman (C)	brave warrior	**Calvert** (OE)	} herdsman
Caesar (L)	purposeful	**Calbert**	
Calder (C)	from the river of stones	**Calvin** (L)	bold
		Cameron (C)	crooked nose

Campbell (F)   from a bright field

Carew (C)   from this fortress

Carey   see Charles

Carl (T)   forceful

Carleton (T)   ⎫
Charleton   ⎬ of Charles' farm

Carlisle (OE)   ⎫
Carlyle   ⎬ from the walled city

Carlos   see Charles

Carmen (L)   song

Carroll (C)   ⎫
Carrol   ⎬ champion

Carson (W)   his father lives near marshes

Carter (OE)   cart-driver

Carver (AS)   carver

Cary (C)   ⎫
Carey   ⎬ from the fortress

Casey (C)   valorous

Casimir (SL)   proclamation of peace

Caspar (Sa)   gift-bearer

Cecil (S)   harmony

Cedric (C)   chieftain

Chadwick (OE)   from the warrior's town; defender

Chandler (F)   candlemaker

Channing (AS)   knowing

Chapin (F)   man of gold

Charles (T)   manly; man of the people

Chauncey (F)   official record-keeper

Chester (OE)   ⎫
Cheston   ⎬ dweller in a fortified town

Chilton (AS)   from the farm by the spring

Christian (L)   Christian

Christopher (G)   Christ-bearer

Clarence (L)   bright; illustrious

Clark (L)   ⎫
Clarke   ⎬ wise

Claude (L)	affectionate	**Constantine** (L)	unwavering
Clay (T)	man of clay or mortal	**Conway** (C)	man of the great plains
Clayton (T)	from the town on the clay bed	**Coolidge** (U)	careful and protective
Clement (L)	merciful	**Corbin** (L)	} the raven
Clifford (Sa)	valorous	**Corwin**	
Clifton (OE)	from the farm at the cliff	**Cornelius** (L)	studious; noble
Clinton (T)	from the headland farm	**Courtland** (AF)	from the enclosed land or court
Clive (OE)	cliff dweller	**Courteney** (F)	a place
Clyde (W)	heard from afar	**Craig** (S)	crag dweller
Colby (OE)	from the black farm	**Crandall** (OE)	of the valley of the cranes
Colin (C)	strong; young and virile	**Crawford** (OE)	of the crow's ford
Coleman (C)	} dove	**Crosby** (T)	dweller by the town cross
Colman			
Columbus (G)	curious	**Culbert** (T)	noted; bright
Conal (C)	} high and mighty	**Culver** (OE)	dove
Conan		**Curt** (L)	short or little
Conrad (T)	bold counsel; resolute	**Curtis** (OF)	courteous
		Cyril (G)	lordly
Conroy (C)	wise	**Cyrus** (P)	throne

D

Dale (T)	dweller in the dale
Dallas (C)	spirited
Dalton (OE)	from the farm in the dale
Damon (G)	tame
Dan (H)	judge
Dana (Sc) **Dane**	} a Dane
Daniel (H)	God has judged
Darcy (C)	dark; dweller in the stronghold
Darius (P)	dark; strong
Darrell (OE) **Daryl** **Darren**	} beloved; dear
David (H)	beloved
Davin (Sc)	bright man
Davis (OE)	contraction of David's son
Dean (OE) **Deane**	} from the valley
Dearborn (AS)	beloved child
Delbert (T)	bright and noble
Delmar (L)	of the sea
Demetrius (G)	lover of the earth
Denby (Sc)	loyal Dane
Denis (G) **Dennis** **Denny**	} worshipper

Derek (T) **Dirk**	} ruler of the people
Desmond (C)	sophisticated
Dewey (U)	controlled physical power
Dexter (L)	fortunate
Dillon (C)	faithful and true
Dion (G)	short for Dionysos, God of wine
Doane (C)	from the sand hill or dune
Dominic (L) **Dominick**	} belonging to the Lord
Don (CL)	dark or brown
Donal (C) **Donald** **Donnie** **Donovan**	} world ruler
Dorian (G)	from Dori
Douglas (C) **Douglass**	} thoughtful
Doyle (C)	dark stranger
Drew (T)	honest
Driscoll (C)	the interpreter
Duane (C)	singing
Dudley (OE)	from the town of Dudley

Duke (L)	leader	Durand (L)	lasting friend
Duncan (C)	brown chief	Durward (AS)	the door
Dunstan (AS)	from the brown		keeper
	stone hill	Dwaine	
Dunton (OE)	of the farm	Dwayne	} see Duane
	over the hill	Dwight (T)	white; fair

E

Earl (OE)	} noble warrior	Eleazar (H)	helped by God
Earle		Eli (H)	highest
Eaton (AS)	of the river	Elias (H)	} faithful
Eben (H)	stone	Elihu	to God
Ebenezer (H)	stone of help	Elijah	
Edan (C)	flame	Ellery (T)	of the
Edgar (OE)	wealthy		alder trees
Edmond (OE)	} protector	Eliot	
Edmund	of wealth	Eliott	} see Elias
Edric (AS)	rich ruler	Elliott	
Edsel (AS)	prosperous	Ellis	
Edward (OE)	guardian	Elson	son of Elias
	of wealth	Ellsworth (AS)	lover of
Edwin (OE)	friend		the earth
	of wealth	Elmer (AS)	excellent;
Egan (T)	formidable		famous
Egbert (T)	precocious;	Elmo (G)	lovable; friendly
	bright	Elroy (L)	royal
Elbert (T)	overpowering;	Elton (AS)	from the
	illustrious		old farm
Elden (T)	} respected	Elvin	see Alvin
Eldon		Elwin (AS)	} friend of
Eldridge (AS)	} wise advisor	Elwood	the elves
Eldwin		Elwyn	

Emmanuel (H)	God is with us	Errol (T)	a nobleman
Emerson (T)	son of Emery	Ervin	} see Irwin
Emery (T)	dutiful	Erwin	
Emil (T)	} industrious	Esmond (AS)	gracious protector
Emile			
Emmett (AS)	} diligence	Ethan (H)	strength; steadfast
Emmet			
Emory (T)	ambitious	Eugene (G)	well-born
Enoch (H)	teacher	Evan (E)	challenger
Enos (H)	mortal man	Evelyn (OE)	a dear youth
Ephraim (H)	very fruitful	Everard	} mighty as a boar
Erasmus (G)	amiable	Everett (T)	
Eric (T)	} princely	Ewald (L)	bearer of good news
Erich			
Erik		Ezekiel (H)	God's strength
Erlànd (T)	noble eagle	Ezra (H)	dawn, beginning of joy
Ernest (G)	serious		

Fabian (L)	prosperous farmer	Fairfax (AS)	fair-haired
		Fairley (AS)	from the far meadow
Fairbanks (U)	sympathetic		

Falkner (AS) Faulkner	} trainer		Fredrick Fredric Fritz	} see Frederick
Farand (T)	attractive		Freeman (AS)	one born free
Farrell (C) Farrel	} man of valor		Fulton (AS)	from a farm
Favian (L)	man of understanding			

Falkner (AS)
Faulkner } trainer

Farand (T) attractive

Farrell (C)
Farrel } man of valor

Favian (L) man of
understanding

Faxon (T) famous for
his hair

Felix (L) fortunate;
happy

Fenton (AS) dweller of
the marshland

Ferdinand (T)
Fernand } adventurous

Fergus (C) strong man

Ferris (C) rock

Firman (AS) traveler to
far places

Fisk (Sc) fisherman

Flavian (L) blond; fair-
haired

Fletcher (F) arrow-
maker

Fleming (AS) Dutchman

Florian (L) flowering

Floyd (C) the gray

Forrest (T)
Forest } from the
woods

Foster (T) keeper of
the woods

Franchot (T) the free

Francis
Frank (T) } free

Franklin (T)
Franklyn } free man

Frederick (T)
Frederic } peaceful ruler

Fredrick
Fredric
Fritz } see Frederick

Freeman (AS) one born free

Fulton (AS) from a farm

Gabriel (H)	man of God	Gerard (T)	mighty with
Gadman (H)	the fortunate		the spear
Gail (C)	} lively, gay	Gervase (T)	honorable
Gale		Gideon (H)	the deliverer
Galen (G)	healer	Gifford (T)	gift
Galvin (C)	the sparrow	Gilbert (T)	bright pledge;
Gamaliel (H)	the Lord		progressive
	is my	Giles (L)	shield bearer
	recompense	Gilroy (L)	king's servant
Garett (T)		Glen (C)	} from the
Gareth	} mighty with		valley
Garreth	the spear	Glenn	or glen
Garrett		Goddard (T)	firm in nature
Garland (OF)	crowned for	Godfrey (T)	quiet
	victory	Goodwin (T)	good and faith-
Garner (T)	the defender;		ful friend
	protecting	Gordon (Ga)	generous
	warrior	Graham (T)	from the
Garnet (L)	red jewel		gray home
Garrick (T)	mighty warrior	Grant (L)	great
Garth (AS)	yard-keeper	Granville (F)	of the great town
Garvin (T)	friend	Gregory (G)	vigilant
	in battle	Griffith (L)	having
Gawain (T)	} battle hawk		great faith
Gavin		Griswold (T)	from the wild
Gaylord (AS)	joyous noble		gray forest
Geoffrey (T)	God's peace;	Grover (AS)	grove-dweller
	brave	Gunther (T)	bold warrior
George (G)	farmer	Gustave (Sc)	noble staff
Gerald (T)	dominion with	Guthrie (C)	war serpent
	the spear	Guy (F)	leader; guide

Hal	see Henry	Heywood (T)	from the dark
Halbert (C)	gentleman		green forest
Hale (T)	robust	Hezekiah (H)	God is strength
Hall (OE)	from the	Hilary (L)	⎱ cheerful;
	master's house	Hillary	⎰ merry
Halsey (AS)	from Hal's island	Hilliard (T)	protector
Hamilton (F)	from the beau-	Hiram (H)	nobly born
	tiful mountain	Holbrook (AS)	from the
Harcourt (F)	from the		valley brook
	armed court	Holden (T)	kind
Hardy (T)	of hardy stock	Hollis (AS)	dweller by the
Harlan (T)	⎱ from the land		holly trees
Harland	⎰ of warriors	Holman (T)	from the
Harley (AS)	from the		river island
	hare's meadow	Homer (G)	pledge; secure
Harod (H)	loud terror		timekeeper;
Harold (AS)	commander of	Horace (L)	worthy to
	the army	Horatio	be beheld
Harrison (S)	noble	Hosea (H)	salvation
Harvey (C)	bitter	Howard (T)	chief guardian
Hayden (T)	from the	Hubert (T)	bright in
	hedged hill		spirit;
Hayes (OE)	from the woods		intellectual
Hector (G)	unswerving;	Hugh (T)	⎱ mind, intel-
	steadfast	Hugo	⎰ ligence
Helmut (G)	helmet of courage	Humbert (T)	bright home
Henry (T)	ruler of the home	Hume (T)	lover of
Herbert (T)	illustrious warrior		his home
Herman (T)	warrior	Humphrey (T)	protector of
Herrod (H)	heroic conqueror		the peace
Herwin (T)	friend	Hyman (H)	life

I

Ian	see John	**Ira** (H)	watchful
Ichabod (H)	the glory has departed	**Irvin** (AS) **Irving**	} friend of the sea
Ignatius (L)	fiery and ardent	**Irwin**	
		Isaac (H)	mirthful; glad
Igor (Sc)	hero	**Isidore** (G)	gift
Ingram (T)	the raven	**Israel** (H)	the Lord's soldier
Inness (C)	from the island		
		Ivar (Sc)	archer

J

Jabez (H)	cause of sorrow	Jerome (G)	having a holy name; exalted
Jack	see John	Jesse (H)	God's grace
Jacob (H)	} the supplanter	Jethro (H)	outstanding
James		Joab (H)	praise the Lord
Jared (H)	descendant	Joachim (H)	the Lord will judge
Jarvis (T)	sharp as a spear	Job (H)	the afflicted
Jason (G)	healer	Jock	see John
Jasper (P)	bringer of treasure	Joel (H)	Jehovah is God
Jay (AS)	crow, or lively	John (H)	} God is gracious; given by God
		Jonathan	
Jeconiah (H)	gift of the Lord	Jonah (H)	place
		Jonas (H)	dove
Jedediah (H)	beloved by the Lord	Jordan (H)	descending
		Joseph (H)	he shall add
Jeffrey	see Geoffrey	Joses (H)	helped by the Lord
Jegar (H)	witness our love	Joshua (H)	Jehovah saves
		Josiah (H)	he is healed by the Lord
Jerald	see Gerald	Jotham (H)	God is perfect
Jeremiah (H)	} exalted by the Lord	Julius (L)	} kind
Jeremy		Julian	
Jermyn		Justin (L)	just

K

Kane (C)	bright; radiant	**Kenneth** (C)	handsome
Karl	see Charles	**Kent** (C)	white or bright
Kay (E)	strong; determined	**Kenway** (AS)	brave soldier
		Kenyon (C)	fair-haired
Keane (OE)	sharp; tall;	**Kermit** (C)	free
Keene	handsome	**Kerr** (C)	dark; mysterious
Keith (W)	wood-dweller		
Kelby (T)	from the farm	**Kerry** (C)	the dark
Kilby	by the spring	**Keary**	
Kelly (U)	impetuous; gentle and helpful	**Kevin** (C)	kind; gentle
		Kimball (AS)	royally brave
		Kingsley (AS)	from the king's meadow
Kelsey (T)	dweller by		
Kelcey	the water	**Kirby** (T)	from the
Kendall (C)	chief of	**Kerby**	church village
Kendal	the valley	**Kirk** (Sc)	living close
Kendrick (AS)	royal ruler		to the church
Kenelm (AS)	bright helmet	**Knute** (Da)	kind
Kenley (OE)	of the king's meadow	**Kyle** (Ga)	fair and handsome

L

Laban (H)	white	**Lamar** (U)	co-operative
Lachlan (C)	warlike	**Lambert** (T)	rich in land
Laird (C)	proprietor	**Lamont** (Sc)	lawyer

Lancelot (AS) / **Lance**	spear
Landon (AS)	from the long hill
Landry (S)	ruler of the place
Lane (AS)	from the country road
Lang (T)	tall
Lathrop (AS)	of the village
Latimer (AS)	Latin teacher
Lawrence (L) / **Laurence**	victorious; crowned with laurels
Lawton (OE)	from the hillside farm
Leander (G)	brave; like a lion
Lear (T)	of the meadow
Lee (AS)	sheltered; meadow
Leighton (OE)	from the meadow farm
Leland (OE)	from the meadow land
Lemuel (H)	dedicated to God
Leo (L) / **Leon** (F)	lion
Leonard (T)	brave or strong as a lion
Leopold (T)	patriotic
Leroy (F)	royal
Leslie (C)	from the gray fort
Lester (AS)	from the army or camp
Levi (H)	a bond or promise
Lewis (T) / **Louis**	famous warrior
Lincoln (C)	from the place by the pool
Linus (H)	flax-haired
Lionel (OF)	a young lion
Llewellyn (C)	lightning
Lloyd (C) / **Loyd**	gray
Lorimer (L)	lover of horses
Loring (T)	from Lorraine
Lot (H)	veiled
Lowell (AS)	beloved
Lucius (L) / **Lucias** / **Lucian**	light
Luther (T)	renowned warrior
Lyle (F)	from the island
Lyman (OE)	man of the plains
Lyndon (OE)	of the linden tree
Lynn (AS)	from the waterfalls
Lysander (G)	liberator

M

Macy (U) enduring material

Maddock (C) fire

Madison (T) mighty in battle

Magnus (L) great

Malcolm (C) servant of St. Columba; dove

Mallory (OE) ill-omened; luckless

Malvin (C) }
Melvin } chief

Manfred (T) peace among men

Manuel see Emmanuel

Marcus (L) }
Mark } martial; defender
Marc }

Marmaduke (C) sea leader

Marsden (AS) from the marsh valley

Marshall (OF) marshal

Martin (L) unyielding

Marvin (T) } famous friend
Marwin } or sea friend

Mason (L) stone worker

Matthew (H) gift of the Lord

Maurice (L) }
Morris } Moorish; dark

Maximilian (L) }
Max } the greatest

Maxwell (AS) dweller by the spring

Maynard (AS) mightily brave

Melville (F)	a place		
Meredith (C)	} protector		
Meridith	} from the sea		
Merle (F)	blackbird		
Merlin (C)	} falcon; hawk		
Marlen	}		
Merrell (T)	}		
Merrill	} famous	Mordecai (H)	wise
Merril	}		counsellor
Merton (AS)	from the place	Morgan (W)	dweller on
	by the sea		the sea
Meyer (T)	farmer	Morley (OE)	from the
Micah (H)	like unto		moor
	the Lord		meadow
Michael (H)	} who is	Morrell (L)	} swarthy
Mitchell	} like God?	Morel	}
Milburn (OE)	from the	Mortimer (F)	ever living
	millstream	Morton (OE)	from the
Miles (L)	} soldier		moor village
Myles	}	Moses (H)	saved from
Millard (OE)	Miller		the water
Milton (AS)	from the	Murdoch (C)	} prosperous
	mill town	Murdock	} seaman
Montague (L)	from the peaked	Murray (C)	} seaman
	mountain	Murry	}
Montgomery (F)	mountain	Myron (G)	} fragrant
	hunter	Myreon	}

Naldo (T)	power	Narcissus (G)	self-loving
Napoleon (G)	lion from	Nash (U)	alert; active
	the forest	Nathan (H)	a gift

Nathaniel (H)	gift of God	**Nicodemus** (G)	the people's conqueror
Neal (C)			
Neil	a champion	**Nigel** (L)	dark
Neill		**Noah** (H)	rest; comfort
Nelson (C)	a son of Neal	**Noel** (FL)	
Nero (L)	black	**Newell**	Christmas
Nestor (G)	venerable wisdom	**Noble** (L)	renowned; noble
Neville (L)	from the new town	**Nolan** (C)	noble or famous
		Noland	
Nevin (AS)	nephew	**Norbert** (T)	shining in the north
Newlin (C)	from the		
Newlyn	new spring	**Norman** (TR)	man from the north
Newton (AS)	from the new estate	**Norris**	see Norman
		Norvin	from the
Nicholas (G)	victorious among the people	**Norton** (AS)	north place
		Norward (T)	guardian of the north gate

Oakes (OE)	the oak	**Olaf** (Sc)	
Oakley (OE)	from the oak tree meadow	**Olin**	peace
		Olen	
Obadiah (H)	Servant of the Lord	**Oliver** (L)	peaceful
Octavius (L)	the eighth	**Omar** (H)	talkative
Odell (T)	wealthy man	**Ordway** (AS)	spear fighter
Odoric (L)	son of a good man	**Oren** (H)	
		Orin	pine
		Orrin	
Ogden (OE)	from the oak valley	**Ormond** (T)	ship man
		Orson (L)	bear

Orville (F)	lord of the manor	**Osmond** (T)	protected by God
Osbert (AS)	divinely bright	**Oswald** (AS)	divine power
Osborn (AS)	divinely strong	**Otis** (G)	keen of hearing
Oscar (OE)	spear of a deity	**Otto** (T)	prosperous
Osgood (T)	gift of our Lord	**Owen** (C)	young warrior

Page (F)	servant to the royal court	**Peregrine** (L)	wanderer
		Perry (OE)	the pear tree
Paige (U)	helpful	**Peter** (G)	a rock; reliable
Paine (L)	country man or rustic	**Pedro** (Sp)	
Payne		**Pierre** (F)	see Peter
Palmer (OE)	palm bearer	**Perrin**	
Park (OE)		**Pierce**	
	keeper of the park •	**Phelan** (C)	brave as a wolf
Parke			
Parker		**Philbert** (T)	radiant soul
Parry (F)	guardian; protector	**Philip** (G)	lover of horses
Pascal (H)	pass over	**Philo** (G)	love
Patrick (L)	noble; patrician	**Phineas** (H)	oracle
		Pierson (OE)	son of Peter
Paul (L)	small	**Pearson**	
Paxton (T)	a traveler; from afar	**Pierpont** (F)	dweller by the stone bridge
Paxon		**Pierrepont**	
Pembroke (OW)	from the headland	**Pius** (L)	pious
		Pollard (T)	cropped hair
Percival (L)	piercing; a knight	**Porter** (L)	doorkeeper; gate keeper
Percy			

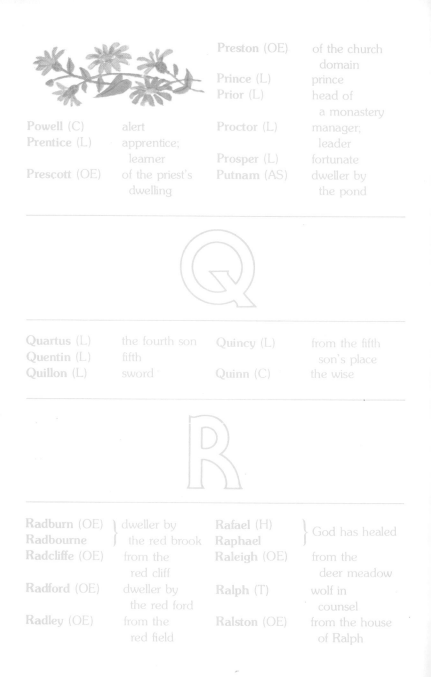

Preston (OE) of the church
domain
Prince (L) prince
Prior (L) head of
a monastery
Powell (C) alert Proctor (L) manager;
Prentice (L) apprentice; leader
learner Prosper (L) fortunate
Prescott (OE) of the priest's Putnam (AS) dweller by
dwelling the pond

Q

Quartus (L) the fourth son Quincy (L) from the fifth
Quentin (L) fifth son's place
Quillon (L) sword Quinn (C) the wise

R

Radburn (OE) } dweller by Rafael (H) } God has healed
Radbourne } the red brook Raphael }
Radcliffe (OE) from the Raleigh (OE) from the
red cliff deer meadow
Radford (OE) dweller by Ralph (T) wolf in
the red ford counsel
Radley (OE) from the Ralston (OE) from the house
red field of Ralph

Ramsey (T)	from the	Remus (L)	oarsman
Ramsay	ram's island	Rene (F)	reborn
Randolph (T)	shielded	Renfred (T)	peacemaker
Randal	or advised	Reuben (H)	behold, a son!
Randall	by wolves	Rex (L)	king
Rawdon (T)	from the	Rexford (LOE)	from the
	deer hill		king's ford
Ray (OF)	kingly	Richard (T)	strong in rule
Rayburn (OE)	from the	Richmond (T)	mighty
Raybourne	deer brook		protector
Raymond (T)	wise pro-	Ridgley (OE)	dweller by
Raymund	tection		meadow's edge
Reade (OE)		Robert (T)	bright in fame
Reid	red-haired	Robin	
Reed		Roderick (T)	famous ruler
Redmond (T)	adviser and	Rodman ((T)	redhead
Redmund	protector	Rodney (T)	renowned
Regan (C)	royal; kingly	Roger (T)	famous
Reginald (T)	wise dominion		spearman

Roland (T)	famous land	**Roy** (L)	king
Rolf		**Royal** (OF)	kingly
Rolfe		**Royce** (F)	son of
Rolph	see Rudolph		the king
Rollin		**Royd** (Sc)	from the for-
Rollo			est clearing
Romeo (L)	pilgrim to Rome	**Royden** (OE)	from the
Romney (L)	a Roman		king's hill
Romulus (L)	citizen of Rome	**Rudolph** (T)	famous wolf
Ronald	see Reginald	**Rudyard** (U)	tenacious
Rory (C)	ruddy;	**Rufus** (L)	red-haired
	red-haired	**Rupert**	see Robert
Roscoe (T)	from the	**Russell** (AS)	like a fox;
	deer forest		red-haired
Ross (T)	horse	**Rutherford** (OE)	from the
Roswald (T)			cattle ford
Roswell	mighty steed	**Ryan** (U)	capable

Salisbury (OE)	from the	**Sandon** (OE)	from the
	guarded		sandy hill
	stronghold	**Sanford** (OE)	from the
Salvador (L)	of the Savior		sandy ford
Samson (H)		**Sargent** (OF)	military
Sampson	like the sun		attendant
Samuel (H)	name of God	**Saul** (H)	asked for
Sanborn (OE)	from the	**Saville** (OF)	from the
	sandy brook	**Savill**	willow farm
Sanders (G)	helper of	**Sawyer** (C)	cutter of
Saunders	mankind		timber

Saxon (T)   from a
     Saxon town

Schuyler (D)   wise man;
     shelter

Scott (S)   wanderer

Seabrook (OE)   from the brook
     by the sea

Searle (T) ⎫ bearing arms;
Serle ⎬   wearing armor
Serlo ⎭

Seaton (OE) ⎫ from the place
Seton ⎭   by the sea

Seaver (AS)   victorious
     stronghold

Sebastian (G)   respected

Sedgewick (OE)   from the village
     of victory

Selby (T)   from the
     manor farm

Selwyn (T)   friend at the
     manor or
     palace

Seth (H)   the chosen or
     appointed

Seward (AS)   defender of
     the coast

Sewell (T)   victorious on
     the sea, mighty
     in victory

Seymour (T)   famed at sea

Shaw (OE)   from the
     shady grove

Shelby (AS)   from the
     ledge farm

Sheldon (AS)   from the
     hill-ledge

Shelley (AS)   from the
     ledge meadow

Shepard (AS) ⎫
Shepherd ⎬ sheep tender
Sheppard ⎭

Shepley (AS)   of the
     sheep meadow

Sherard (AS)   valiant soldier

Sheridan (C)   wild man

Sherlock (OE)   fair haired son

Sherman (AS)   wool-shearer
     or cutter

Sherwin (AS)   a true friend

Sherwood (OE)   from the
     bright forest

Sibley (AS)   friendly

Sidney (F) ⎫ follower of
Sydney ⎭ St. Denis

Simpson   see Samson

Siegfried (T)   victorious
     peace

Sigmund (T)   victorious
     protection

Silas (L) ⎫
Silvanus ⎪
Sylvanus ⎬ of the woods
Silvester ⎪
Sylvester ⎭

Simeon (H)   servant of
     the Lord

Simon (H)   obedient

Sinclair (L)   illustrious

Sion (H)   exalted

Sloan (C) ⎫
Sloane ⎭ warrior

Sol (L)   the sun

Solomon (H)   peaceable

Spencer (OEL) ⎫ storekeeper;
Spenser ⎬ dispenser of
    ⎭ provisions

Sprague (OE)	alert; quick			

Stanton (AS) — from the stone dwelling

Stanway (OE) — dweller by the stone highway

Stanwood (OE) — from the stony wood

Stephen (G) **Steven** } crown

Sprague (OE) — alert; quick

Stacey (L) **Stacy** } stable; dependable

Sterling (T) **Stirling** } good value; genuine

Stafford (OE) — from the landing ford

Stewart (AS) **Stuart** } keeper of the estate

Standish (OE) — from the stony park

Stillman (AS) — quiet; gentle

Stanfield (OE) — from the stony field

Stillwell (AS) — from the still spring

Stanhope (OE) — from the stony hollow

Stoddard (OE) — keeper of horses

Stanislaus (SI) — glory of the camp

Sumner (OFL) — summoner

Sutton (OE) — from the south village or town

Stanley (OE) — dweller by the stony sea

Swaine (T) — boy

T

Taber (OF) — herald

Teague (C) — poet

Tait (T) **Tate** } cheerful

Tearle (OE) — stem

Tedman (T) **Tedmund** } protector of the nation

Talbott (AS) — bloodhound

Tavis (C) — son of David

Terence (L) **Terrence** } tender

Taylor (L) — a tailor

Valerian (L)	strong	**Vere** (L)	true
Vance (T)	son of a	**Vernon** (L)	flourishing
	famous family	**Victor** (L)	conqueror
Vandyke (T)	of the dyke	**Vincent** (L)	conquering
Van Ness (T)	of the		one
	headland	**Vinson** (AS)	son of Vinn
Varden (FC)	from the	**Virgil** (L)	strong;
Vardon	green hill		flourishing
Varian (L)	clever;	**Vito** (L)	vital
	capricious	**Vivien** (L)	lively
Vaughan (C)	small or	**Vladimir** (Sl)	world ruler
Vaughn	little	**Volney** (T)	most popular

Wade (AS)	wanderer	**Ward** (AS)	guardian
Wadsworth (OE)	from Wade's	**Ware** (AS)	careful;
	castle		prudent
Walcott (OE)	dweller in	**Warfield** (OE)	from the field
Walcot	the walled		by the dam
	cottage	**Waring** (AS)	cautious
Waldemar (T)	strong and	**Warner** (T)	protecting
	famous		warrior
Waldon (OE)	from the	**Warren** (T)	protecting
	wooded hill		friend
Waldron (T)	mighty raven	**Warwick** (T)	strong ruler
Walker (OE)	forester	**Warrick**	
Wallace (T)	foreigner	**Warton** (OE)	from the poplar-
Walter (T)	powerful; of		tree farm
	great destiny	**Washburn** (U)	regard for
Walton (OE)	from the		convention
	enclosed	**Washington** (Sa)	purifying
	farmstead	**Watson** (AS)	warrior's son

Wayland (OE)	from the land by the highway	**Whitby** (AS)	from the white dwellings
Wayne (OE)	wagon-maker	**Whitelaw** (AS)	of the white hill
Webster (OE)	weaver		
Welby (OE)	from the farm by the spring	**Whitney** (AS)	from the white island
Weldon (OE)	from the spring by the hill	**Wilburn** (AS)	inventive
		Wiatt	see Wyatt
Wellington (AS)	from the prosperous estate	**Wilber**	see Wilburn
		Wildon (OE)	from the wooded hill
Wells (OE)	dweller by the spring	**Wilfred** (T) **Wilfrid**	} desired peace
Wendell (T) **Wendel**	} wanderer	**Willard** (Sa) **William** (T)	protecting determined protector
Wescott (AS)	dwells at the west cottage	**Willis**	son of William
Wesley (AS) **Wellesley** **Westley**	} from the west meadow	**Wilmer** (T) **Wilmar**	} beloved and famous
		Wilmot (T)	beloved heart
Weston (OE)	from the west village	**Wilson** (T)	son of William
Weylin (C)	son of the wolf	**Wilton** (OE)	from the farmstead by the spring

Tramayne (C) **Tremain**	} from the town of the stone
Trent (L)	swift
Trevor (C)	prudent traveler
Tristram (L) **Tristan**	} sorrowful
Truman (AS)	a faithful man

Tudor (G)	divine gift
Turner (L)	worker with the lathe
Tybalt (T)	leader of the people
Tyler (OE)	maker of tiles
Tyson (T)	son of the German

Udo (U)	sacrifices personal comfort for general good
Uland (T)	from the noble land
Ulric (T) **Ulrick**	} ruler of all
Ulysses (L)	venturer

Unni (H)	modest
Upton (AS)	from the high town
Urban (L)	from the city; sophisticated
Uriah (H)	the Lord is my light
Urian (G)	from heaven
Uziel (H)	a mighty force

Vachel (F)	keeper of the cattle
Valdis (T)	spirited in battle

Vale (FL) **Vail**	} from the valley
Valentine (L)	healthy; strong; valorous

Terrill (T)   martial;
                       belonging
                       to Thor
Tertius (L)   the third
Thaddeus (H)   praise to God
Thatcher (AS) ⎤
Thacher   ⎬   mender of
Thaxter   ⎦   roofs
Thayer (T)   of the
                       nation's army
Theodore (G)   gift of God
Theodric (T)   the people's
                       ruler
Theron (G)   hunter
Thomas (H)   the twin;
                       good company
Thor (Sc)   thunderous one
Thornton (AS)   from the thorn
                       tree place
Thorpe (AS)   from the
                       small village
Thurlow (Sc)   from Thor's
                       mountain
Thurman (Sc)   under Thor's
                       protection
Thurston (Sc)   Thor's stone
Tilden (OE)   from the fer-
                       tile valley
Tilford (OE)   from the
                       fertile ford
Timothy (G)   revering God
Tirrell   see Terrill
Titus (L)   saved
Tobias (H) ⎤
Tobin   ⎦   God's goodness
Todd (L)   the fox
Toland (AS)   from the
                       taxed land

Tolman (AS)   collector
                       of taxes
Torrance   see Terence
Torrey (C)   dweller by
                       the forest
Townsend (AS)   from the end
                       of the town
Tracey (AS) ⎤   brave
Tracy   ⎦   defender
Trahern (C)   stronger
                       than iron
Travers (OFL) ⎤   from the
Travis   ⎦   crossroad

Winchell (AS)	drawer of water	**Woodley** (OE)	from the wooded meadow
Winfield (AS)	from the friendly field	**Woodrow** (OE)	from the hedgerow by the forest
Windsor (T)	} at the bend of the river	**Woodward** (OE)	keeper of the forest
Winsor			
Winfred (T)	} joyous peace	**Worden** (OE)	guardian
Winfrid		**Worthington** (AS)	from the riverside
Winslow (AS)	friendly		
Winston (AS)	from the friendly town	**Wright** (OE)	craftsman
		Wyatt (OE)	guide
Winthrop (AS)	from the friendly village	**Wylie** (AS)	beguiling
		Wyman (AS)	warrior
Wirt (AS)	worthy	**Wyndham** (OE)	from the windy village
Wolfe (T)	wolf		
Wolfram (T)	respected; feared	**Wynne** (U)	intuitive; sympathetic
Wolfgang (T)	path of a wolf		

X

Xavier (A)	brilliant
Xenos (G)	stronger
Xerxes (P)	king

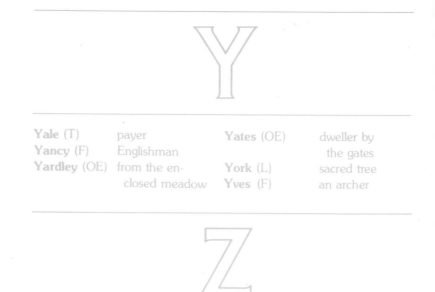

Y

Yale (T)   payer
Yancy (F)   Englishman
Yardley (OE)   from the en-
              closed meadow

Yates (OE)   dweller by
              the gates
York (L)   sacred tree
Yves (F)   an archer

Z

Zaccheus (H)   pure
Zachariah (H)   ⎫
Zacharias   ⎬ God has
Zachary   ⎭ remembered
Zebadiah (H)   the Lord's
               gift

Zebedee (H)   a blessing
Zebulon (H)   dwelling place
Zelig (T)   blessed
Zenas (G)   gift of Zeus
Zephaniah (H)   the Lord has
               hidden

Abigail (H)	source of joy	**Alda** (T)	rich
Ada (H)	joyous	**Aldercy** (OE)	chief or prince
Adabel (T)	} happy and fair	**Aldis** (OE)	} from the
Adabelle		**Aldys**	house
Adah (H)	ornament	**Aldora** (G)	winged gift
Adalia (T)	noble	**Alethea** (G)	picturesque
Adela (T)		**Alexandra** (G)	} helper of
Adelaide	} of noble rank	**Alexis**	mankind
Adele		**Alfreda** (T)	supernaturally
Adiel (H)	ornament of		wise
	the Lord	**Alice** (T)	
Adine (H)	} delicate	**Alicia**	}
Adina		**Allis**	noble
Adna (H)	pleasure	**Alyse**	
Adora (T)	the beloved	**Alison**	
Adria (L)	the unknown	**Alida** (G)	from the city
Adrienne (L)	woman of		of fine vest-
	the sea		ments
Agatha (G)	good	**Allegra** (L)	cheerful
Agnes (G)	pure, chaste	**Alma** (L)	cherishing
Aida	see Ada	**Almira** (A)	princess
Aileen (G)	light	**Alodie** (AS)	wealthy, pros-
Ailsa (T)	of good		perous
	cheer	**Aloyse** (T)	} famous in
Aimee (F)	beloved	**Aloysia**	battle
Airlia (G)	ethereal	**Alta** (L)	high
Alana (C)	} fair, comely	**Althea** (G)	wholesome,
Alanna			healing
Alarice (T)	ruler of all	**Alva** (L)	white
Alberta (T)	noble and	**Alvina** (T)	beloved;
	brilliant		friend of all

Alvita (L)	vivacious	Amaryllis (G)	fresh, sparkling
Alysia (G)	captivating	Amber (A)	a jewel
Alyssa (T)	noble; of good cheer	Amelia (T)	industrious
Amabel (L)	lovable	Amena (C)	honest
Amanda (L)	worthy to be loved	Amethyst (G)	sober
		Amity (L)	friendly
Amara (G)	unfading	Amorette (L)	little love; sweetheart
Amaris (H)	whom God has promised	Amy (L)	beloved

Amaryllis (G) fresh, sparkling
Amber (A) a jewel
Amelia (T) industrious
Amena (C) honest
Amethyst (G) sober
Amity (L) friendly
Amorette (L) little love; sweetheart
Amy (L) beloved
Anastasia (G) one who will rise again
Anatola (G) of the east
Andrea (It) womanly
Angela (G) ⎫
Angelica   ⎬ angel; heavenly messenger
Angelina   ⎭
Anita (Sp) form of Ann
Ann (H) full of grace
Anna ⎫
Anne ⎬ see Ann
Annette ⎭
Anselma (T) protectress
Anthea (G) like a flower
Antonia (L) super excellent; incomparable
Antoinette (F) see Antonia
Aphrodite (G) goddess of love
April (L) to open
Arabella (L) fair and beautiful
Araminta (H) lofty
Ardath (AS) ⎫
Ardith   ⎬ rich gift
Ardis (L) ⎫
Ardra   ⎬ fervent; eager
Aretina (G) virtuous

		Astrid (Sc)	beautiful as a goddess
		Atalaya (SpA)	a watch tower
		Atalie (Sw)	pure
		Athena (G)	wisdom
		Audrey (OE)	noble strength
		Audris (T)	fortunate
		Augusta (L)	majestic, exalted
Ariadne (G)	holy one		
Ariana (W)	silvery	Aurelia (L)	golden
Arlene (C)		Avis (L)	
Arleen	} a pledge	Ava	} a bird
Arlana		Azalia (H)	whom the Lord has spared
Ariella (H)	ethereal		
Astra (G)	like a star		

B

Babette (F)	dim. of Elizabeth	Bernardine (T)	} brave; strong
		Bernadette	
Barbara (G)	mysterious; foreign	Bernice (G)	bringing victory
Bathsheba (H)	daughter of our oath	Bertha (T)	bright
		Bertilde (T)	commanding
Beata (L)	blessed	Beryl (H)	jewel
Beatrice (L)	she brings joy	Bess	
Belinda (E)	shining, bright	Bessie	
		Betsy	
Belle (F)	beautiful	Bette	} see Elizabeth
Bena (H)	wise	Bettina	
Benita (L)		Betty	
Benedicta	} the blessed	Beth	

Beulah (H)	married	**Bonita** (Sp)	pretty
Beverly (AS)	beaver meadow	**Brenda** (T)	fiery
Blanche (OF) **Bianca**	white; fair	**Brenna** (C)	maiden with raven hair
Blenda (T)	dazzling, glorious	**Briana** (C)	the strong
		Bridget (C) **Bridgette**	strong
Blythe (AS)	happy, joyous		
Bonnie (OE)	pretty, sweet	**Brunhilde** (T)	battle heroine

Calandra (G)	the lark	**Cary** (C) **Carey**	dark of hair or complexion
Camilla (L) **Camille**	noble, self-sacrificing	**Cassandra** (G)	prophetess
Candace (L) **Candida** **Candice**	pure, glowing	**Catharine** **Catherine** **Cathleen**	see Katherine
Cara (C)	friend	**Cecilia** (L) **Cecile** **Cecily** **Celia**	musical
Carin (L) **Caryn** **Carina**	the keel		
Carla (T)	one who is strong	**Celeste** (L) **Celesta** **Celestine**	heavenly
Carlene **Carleen** **Carlin**	see Caroline	**Chandra** (San)	she outshines the stars
Carlotta (Sp)	noble birth	**Charissa** (G)	graceful
Carmel (H)	garden land	**Charity** (L)	charitable, loving
Carmen (L)	song	**Charlotte** (T) **Charlene**	strong; noble-spirited
Carol (OF)	song of joy		
Caroline (T) **Carolyn** **Carrie**	one who is strong	**Charmaine** (L)	little song
		Cherie (F) **Cheryl**	dear one

Chloe (G)	blossoming	Clotilde (T)	famous battle
Christa (G)	Christian	Clothilda	maiden
Christine (G)	fair Christian	Clyte (G)	a nymph
Clara (L)	bright, clear	Colette (G)	victorious
Claire		Collette	
Clarabelle (L)	bright, shining	Colleen (Ga)	girl
		Constance (L)	unchanging; loyal
Clarissa (L)	making famous		
Clarice		Consuela (L)	consolation
Claudia (L)	dazzling	Cora (G)	maiden
Claudette		Corinne	
Clematis (G)	clinging	Cordelia (L)	sincere
Clementine (L)	kind, merciful	Cornelia (L)	womanly virtue
Cleopatra (G)	famous	Crystal (G)	pure
Cleo		Cynthia (G)	moon goddess

Dagmar (Da)	joy of the land	Darlene (AS)	dearly beloved
Daisy (E)	daisy	Darleen	
Dale (T)	dweller in the valley	Darline	
		Daryl (OE)	beloved, dear
Dama (L)	lady	Davina (H)	loved one
Damara (G)	gentle girl	Dawn (AS)	break of day
Daphne (G)	laurel	Deanna	see Diana
Dara (H)	the heart of wisdom	Deborah (H)	industrious
		Decima (L)	the tenth
Darcie (FC)	from the stronghold	Deidre (Ga)	sorrowful
Darcey		Delia (G)	from Delos
Darda (H)	pearl of wisdom	Della	
		Delilah (H)	temptress; coquette
Darice (P)	queenly		

Devona (AS) — the defender

Diana (L) ⎫
             ⎬ moon goddess;
Diane   ⎭ perfect

Dinah (H) ⎫
           ⎬ judgment
Dina   ⎭

Dione (G) — daughter of heaven and earth

Dolores (L) — Our Lady of Sorrows

Dominica (L) ⎫ born on the
Dominique   ⎭ Lord's day

Donella (L) — little mistress

Donna (L) — lady

Dora (G) — gift

Dorcas (G) — gazelle

Dorinda (G) — bountiful gift

Doris (G) ⎫
           ⎬ sea goddess
Doria   ⎭

Dorothy (G) ⎫
             ⎬ God's gift
Dorothea   ⎭

Drusilla (G) — soft-eyed

Dulcie (L) — sweet, charming

Delora (L) ⎫ from the
            ⎬ seashore
Delores   ⎭ see Dolores

Delphine (G) — calm; serene

Demetria (G) — from the fertile land

Denise (G) ⎫
            ⎬ worshipper
Denys   ⎭

Desdemona (G) — girl of sadness

Desiree (FL) — hoped-for

Desma (G) — pledge or bond

E

Echo (G) — a Greek nymph

Edana (C) — fiery; ardent

Eden (H) — delightful; enchanting

Edith (T) ⎫ rich gift;
           ⎬ stately
Editha   ⎭

Edlyn (AS) — of the nobility

Edna (G)	delight	Endora (H)	fountain
Edwina (AS)	valued friend	Enid (C)	quiet; pure
Effie (G)	fair and famed	Erica (Sc)	of royalty
Eileen	} see Aileen	Erina (C)	girl from Ireland
Elaine (G)	light; bright		
Elberta	see Alberta	Ernestine (T)	purposeful; earnest
Eleanor (G)	} light		
Eleanora		Esmerelda (G)	emerald
Elena		Estelle (L)	a star
Elinor	} see Helen	Esther (H)	a star
Ella		Ethel (T)	noble
Ellen		Eudora (G)	wonderful or delightful gift
Electra (G)	shining star		
Elfreda (T)	noble and wise	Eugenia (G)	well-born
Elizabeth (H)		Eunice (G)	bringing a happy victory
Elisabeth			
Elsa			
Elsia	} promised by God	Euphemia (G)	accomplished; famed
Elise			
Eliza		Eurydice (G)	broad separation
Elsbeth			
Elma (G)	pleasant	Evadne (G)	fortunate; faithful
Eloise (OF)	romantic		
Elva (T)	elf	Evangeline (G)	bearer of good news
Elvira (Sp)	like an elf		
Emily (T)	} industrious	Eve (H)	
Emilia		Eva	} life
Emma (T)	one who heals	Evelyn	
Emmeline (E)	intellectual	Evita	

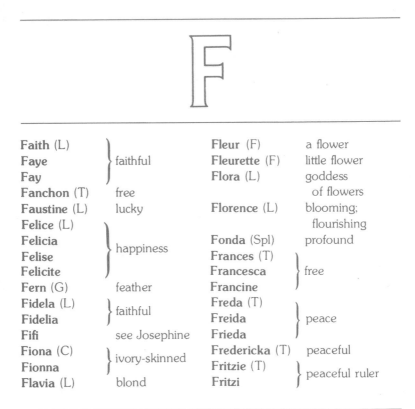

F

Faith (L)	⎫	**Fleur** (F)	a flower
Faye	⎬ faithful	**Fleurette** (F)	little flower
Fay	⎭	**Flora** (L)	goddess
Fanchon (T)	free		of flowers
Faustine (L)	lucky	**Florence** (L)	blooming;
Felice (L)	⎫		flourishing
Felicia	⎬ happiness	**Fonda** (Spl)	profound
Felise	⎬	**Frances** (T)	⎫
Felicite	⎭	**Francesca**	⎬ free
Fern (G)	feather	**Francine**	⎭
Fidela (L)	⎫ faithful	**Freda** (T)	⎫
Fidelia	⎭	**Freida**	⎬ peace
Fifi	see Josephine	**Frieda**	⎭
Fiona (C)	⎫ ivory-skinned	**Fredericka** (T)	peaceful
Fionna	⎭	**Fritzie** (T)	⎫
Flavia (L)	blond	**Fritzi**	⎬ peaceful ruler

Gail	⎫	**Gay** (F)	merry
Gayle	⎬ see Abigail	**Gemini** (G)	⎫ twin
Gale	⎭	**Gemima**	⎭
Gabrielle (H)	woman of God	**Georgiana** (G)	⎫
Garnet (T)	radiant	**Georgia**	⎬ earth-lover
	red jewel	**Georgette**	⎭

Geraldine (T)	affectionate	Glenna (Ga)	
Gerda (T)	the protected	Glenda	} from the glen
Germaine (F)	exquisite	Glynis	
Gertrude (T)	strength of	Gloria (L)	glorious
	a spear	Grace (L)	favor; grace
Gilberta (T)	bright pledge	Greer (G)	watchwoman
Gilda (C)	God's servant	Greta	
Giselle (T)	} pledge or	Gretchen	} see Margaret
Gisela	} promise	Griselda (T)	heroine
Gittel (H)	maiden of	Guinevere (C)	fair lady
	the winepress	Gwendolyn (C)	
Gladys (W)	demure;	Gwendolen	} white-browed; fair
	delicate	Gwynne	

Hagar (H)	flight	Henrietta (T)	ruler of the house
Hannah (H)	grace;	Hephzibah (H)	my joy is in her
	compassion	Hera (G)	Greek Queen
Harriet (T)			of the Gods
Harrietta	} mistress of	Hermione (G)	of the earth
Hatty	} the home	Hesper (G)	evening star
Hazel (AS)	authority	Hester (P)	a star
Heartha (T)	earth mother	Hilary (L)	cheerful
Heather (AS)	the heather	Heloise	see Louise
Hedda (T)	war	Hilda (T)	
Hedwig (T)	storm; strife	Hildegarde	} strong
Helen (G)	} light	Holly (AS)	the holly
Helena	}	Honora (L)	honorable
Helga (T)	holy	Hope (AS)	hope
Helsa (H)	given to God	Hortense (L)	garden worker

I

Ianthe (G)	delightful	**Ingrid**	see Inga
Ida (T)	} happy	**Iona** (G)	purple jewel
Idette		**Irene** (G)	peace
Idelia (T)	noble	**Iris** (G)	a rainbow
Idola (G)	vision	**Irma** (T)	strong
Idona (T)	industrious	**Isabel**	
Ignacia (L)	ardent	**Isabelle**	} see Elizabeth
Ilka (TL)	hard worker	**Isobel**	
Imogene (L)	image	**Isadora** (G)	a gift
Ina (G)	pure	**Isolde** (C)	fair
Inez (Sp)	chaste	**Ivah** (H)	} God's gracious
Inga (Sc)	a daughter	**Ivana**	gift

J

Jacinta (G)	beautiful; comely	**Jennifer** (C)	white wave
Jacqueline (H)	the supplanter	**Jessica** (H)	grace of God
Jada (H)	} wise	**Joan** (H)	} God's gracious
Jadda		**Joann**	gift
Jane (H)		**Joanna**	
Janet	} God's grace		
Janice			
Jenny			
Jean	} see Joan		
Jeannette			

Johanna	see Joan	Julia (L)	
Jobina (H)	the afflicted	Juliana	
Jocelyn (L)	fair; merry	Juliet	} youthful
Josephine (H)	she shall add	Jill	
Joy (OF)	delight	June (L)	young
Joyce (OF)	joyful	Justine (L)	
Judith (H)	praise of the Lord	Justa	} the just

Kara
Karen   } see Katherine
Karin

Katherine (G)
Katharine
Kathryn   } pure
Katrina
Kitty

Kay (G)   rejoicing
Kendra (AS)   the knowing
               woman
Kirby (AS)   from the
               church
               town
Kirsten (Sc)   the anointed
               one

Koren (G)   young girl
Kyla (Ga)   comely

L

Lalita (San)	artless	Lillian (L)	
Lana (C)	handsome	Lila	pure as a
Lara (L)	well-known	Lilian	lily
Laura (L)		Lilyan	
Laurel		Lillith (H)	evil woman
Laureen	the laurel;	Lily	see Lillian
Lora	famous	Lilybelle	
Loretta		Linda (Sp)	beautiful
Lorna		Lisa (H)	consecrated
Laverne (F)	springlike	Liza	to God
Lavinia (L)	woman of Rome	Lois	see Louise
Leah (H)	the weary	Lola	see Charlotte
Lea		Lorelei (T)	temptress
Lee (AS)	meadow	Lorraine (T)	famous in battle
Leila (Ar)	black, dark as night	Lotus (Egypt)	bloom of forgetfulness
Lenore	see Helen	Louise (T)	romantic
Leona (L)	the lion	Lucy (L)	light
Leonie		Lucille	
Leontine (L)	brave as	Lucia	see Lucy
Leora	a lion	Lucinda	
Leslie (C)	from the	Luella (L)	the appeaser
Lesley	gray fort	Luna (L)	the moon
Leta (L)	joy; delight	Lydia (G)	intelligent
Letitia		Lynne (AS)	cascade
Libby (H)	consecrated to God	Lynna	
		Lyris (G)	lyrical
Lida (Sl)	loved by all		
Lyda			

Mabel (L)	} lovable	**Martha** (Ar)	} the lady
Maybelle		**Marta**	
Madeline (H)	} tower of strength	**Martina** (L)	belonging to Mars
Madeleine			
Madelyn		**Mary** (H)	
Madra (L)	mother	**Marie**	bitter; sympathetic
Mae (ME)	} maiden	**Moira**	
May		**Molly**	
Magda	see Madeleine	**Mathilda** (T)	} courageous
Maida (AS)	maiden	**Maude**	
Malina (H)	from a high tower	**Maureen** (L)	} dark
		Maurita	
Mamie	see Mary	**Mavis** (C)	songbird
Mara	see Mary	**Maxine** (L)	the greatest
Marcella (L)	} of Mars	**Medea** (G)	part goddess
Marcia		**Megan** (C)	} the strong
Margaret (G)		**Meghan**	
Margery		**Mehetabel** (H)	one of God's favored
Margot	} a pearl		
Marjorie		**Melanie** (G)	blackness
Marquerite		**Melinda** (Sa)	grateful
Marian		**Melissa** (G)	honey bee
Marie		**Melodie** (G)	song
Marion	} see Mary	**Melvina** (C)	chief
Marietta		**Mercedes** (Sp)	merciful
Marina (L)	sea maiden	**Meredith** (C)	protector of the sea
Maris (L)	sea star		
Marleen	} see Madeline	**Merle** (L)	} blackbird
Marlene		**Meryl**	
Marsha	see Marcia	**Merritt** (AS)	of merit

Meta (L)	ambitious	**Minerva** (G)	} wise
Mia (L)	mine	**Minnie**	
Michele (F) }	who is like	**Minna** (T)	loving memory
Michelle	God	**Mirabel** (L)	of great
Mignon (OF)	dainty		beauty
Mildred (OF)	gentle	**Miranda** (L)	to be admired
	strength	**Miriam** (H)	see Mary
Millicent (T)	strength	**Mitzie**	see Margaret
Mimi (T)	resolute	**Modesta** (L)	shy
	opponent	**Moira** }	see Mary
		Mollie	
		Mona (Ga)	solidarity
		Monica (L)	advisor
		Morla (H)	chosen by
			the Lord
		Morna (Ga)	tender and
			gentle
		Moya (C)	the great
		Muriel (H)	bittersweet
		Myra (L)	wonderful
		Myrtle (G)	victorious
			crown

Nadine (F) }	hope	**Narda** (P)	anointed
Nada		**Natalie** (L) }	child of
Nan		**Nathalie**	Christmas
Nancy }	see Ann	**Natasha**	
Nanette		**Neda** (Sl)	Sunday's child
Nanna (H) }	grace	**Nelda** (OE)	of the elder
Nana			tree
Naomi (H)	pleasant	**Nerine** (G)	sea nymph

Nerissa (G)	of the sea
Nicole (G)	victory of
Nicolette	the people
Nichola	

Niobe (G)	tearful
Noel (L)	Christmas child
Nola (C)	noble; famous
Nona (L)	the ninth
Nora	see Eleanor,
Norah	Helen
Noreen	see Honora
Norma (L)	model
Nydia (L)	a refuge

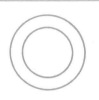

Octavia (L)	the eighth one
Odele (G)	melody
Odelia (T)	prosperous
Odette (F)	home lover
Ola (Sc)	daughter or descendant
Olga (T)	holy
Olivia (L)	olive; peace-
Olive	bringer
Olympia (G)	of the mountain of the Gods
Opal (San)	jewel
Ophelia (G)	wise
Oriana (L)	golden
Oribel (L)	golden beauty
Oriole (L)	golden thrush
Oriel	
Orlena (L)	golden
Orna (I)	olive-colored
Ottilie (T)	battle heroine

P

Paige (AS)	} young; child	**Petra** (G)	rock
Page		**Petrina** (G)	steadfast
Pamela (G)	honey; loving	**Petula** (OF)	} peevish
Pandora (G)	gifted	**Petulah**	
Pansy (F)	thought	**Phenice** (H)	from a palm tree
Patience (L)	patient	**Philana** (G)	friend of
Patricia (L)	} of the		mankind
Patty	nobility;	**Philippa** (G)	lover of horses
Patsy	well-born	**Philomena** (G)	loving friend
Paula (L)	} little	**Phoebe** (G)	shining
Paulette		**Phyllis** (G)	green leaf
Pauline		**Pia** (L)	devout
Pearl (E)	pearl	**Polly**	see Mary
Pegeen (C)	pearl	**Pomona** (L)	fragrant
Penelope (G)	weaver;	**Poppy**	from the poppy
	industrious	**Portia** (L)	doorway
Peony (G)	flower	**Prima** (L)	first born
Pepita (Sp)	she shall add	**Primrose** (L)	first rose
Perdita (L)	lost	**Priscilla** (L)	of long lineage
Persephone (G)	} weaver of	**Prudence** (L)	prudent
Persis	dreams	**Psyche** (G)	soul

Q

Queena (OE)	woman; queen	**Questa** (L)	seeker
Quenby (Sc)	wife; womanly	**Quinta** (L)	fifth child
Querida (Sp)	loved one	**Quirita** (L)	citizen

Rachel (H)		**Roberta** (AS)	of shining
Rae	ewe; motherly	**Robin**	fame
Ray		**Roderica** (T)	princess
Ramona (T)	protector	**Rolanda** (T)	famous
Rana (San)	royal	**Roma** (L)	woman of Rome
Raina		**Ronalda** (T)	powerful
Raphaela (H)	blessed healer	**Rosabel** (L)	beautiful rose
Rebba (H)	fourth child	**Rosalie** (L)	festival of roses
Rebecca (H)	tie; bond	**Rosalind** (L)	fair rose
Reba		**Roslyn**	
Regina (L)	queenly	**Rosanne** (L)	gracious rose
Renata	see Irene	**Rose** (L)	rose
Rene		**Rosa**	
Renita (L)	poised; firm	**Rosamond**	
Renee (F)	reborn	**Rosemarie** (L)	Mary's rose
Rhea (G)	motherly	**Rowena** (C)	flowing fair hair
Rhoda (G)	rose	**Roxana** P)	dawn
Rita (G)	pearl	**Roxanne**	
Riva (OF)	dreamer	**Ruby** (OF)	red
Roanna (L)	sweet; gracious	**Ruth** (H)	friend

Sabrina (AS)	a princess	**Salena** (G)	salty
Sacha (G)	helpmate	**Salome** (H)	woman of
Sadie	see Sarah		perfection
Sallie		**Samara** (H)	watchful; cautious

Samuela (H) } **Samantha** }	name of God	**Sophia** (G) **Sonia** **Sonya** }	wisdom
Sandra (G)	helper of mankind	**Stella** (L)	star
Sarah (H)	princess	**Stephanie** (G) } **Stephenie** }	crown
Selena (G)	moon-goddess		
Selma (C)	fair	**Susan** (H) } **Susanna** }	lily
Seraphine (H)	deeply religious		
Serena (L)	tranquil	**Susanne** **Suzette** }	see Susan
Sharon (H)	of the land of Sharon	**Sybil** (G)	prophetess
Sheila (C)	musical	**Sydel** (H)	enchantress
Shirley (AS)	from the white meadow	**Sydney** (H)	the enticer
Simone (H)	heard by the Lord	**Sylvia** (L) } **Silvia** }	forest maiden

T

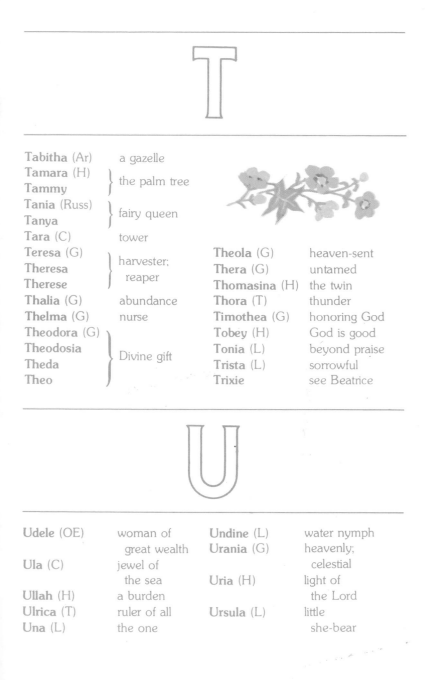

Tabitha (Ar)	a gazelle
Tamara (H)	} the palm tree
Tammy	
Tania (Russ)	} fairy queen
Tanya	
Tara (C)	tower
Teresa (G)	} harvester; reaper
Theresa	
Therese	
Thalia (G)	abundance
Thelma (G)	nurse
Theodora (G)	} Divine gift
Theodosia	
Theda	
Theo	

Theola (G)	heaven-sent
Thera (G)	untamed
Thomasina (H)	the twin
Thora (T)	thunder
Timothea (G)	honoring God
Tobey (H)	God is good
Tonia (L)	beyond praise
Trista (L)	sorrowful
Trixie	see Beatrice

U

Udele (OE)	woman of great wealth	**Undine** (L)	water nymph
Ula (C)	jewel of the sea	**Urania** (G)	heavenly; celestial
Ullah (H)	a burden	**Uria** (H)	light of the Lord
Ulrica (T)	ruler of all	**Ursula** (L)	little she-bear
Una (L)	the one		

Valda (T)	battle heroine	Verna (L)	spring-born
Valentina (L)	vigorous	Veronica (L)	true image
Valerie (L)	strong	Vesta (L)	guardian of the
Vanessa (G)	butterfly		sacred fire
Vania (H)	God's gracious gift	Victoria (L)	
		Victorine	} victorious
Vashti (H)	fairest; loveliest	Vida (HL)	beloved
		Vinna (OE)	of the vine
Veda (San)	wise	Violet (L)	
Velda (T)	of great wisdom	Viola	} shy; modest
		Virginia (L)	pure; chaste
Velma (T)	warm-hearted	Vita (L)	life
Vera (Russ)	faith	Vivian (L)	
Verda (L)	young; fresh	Vivienne	} lively

Wallis (T)	girl of Wales	Wilfreda (T)	resolute peacemaker
Wanda (T)	wanderer		
Wenona (Am. Indian)	the first born	Wilhelmina (T)	protectress
		Willa (AS)	desired; desirable
Wilda (AS)	untamed wild one	Wilma (T)	determined
Wileen (T)	resolute protectress	Winifred (T)	friend of peace
		Wynne (C)	fair; white

X

Xanthe (G)	blonde	**Xena** (G)	
Xantippe (G)	shrewish	**Xenia**	} hospitable
		Xylia (G)	of the wood

Y

Yetta (T)	mistress of	**Yvonne** (F)	
	the house	**Yvette**	} the archer
Yolande (L)	} modest; shy		
Yolanda			

Z

Zabrina (AS)	of the nobility	**Zerlina** (T)	serenely
Zandra (G)	helper of		beautiful
	mankind	**Zillah** (H)	restful
Zaneta (H)	God's gracious	**Zinah** (H)	abundance
	gift	**Zipporah** (H)	bird
Zebada (H)	gift of the Lord	**Zita** (G)	harvester
Zenda (P)	womanly	**Zoe** (G)	life
Zena (G)		**Zora** (L)	
Zenia	} hospitable	**Zorah**	} dawn
Zenobia (G)	} having life	**Zorana**	
	from Jupiter	**Zuleika** (A)	fair

Set in Souvenir by Northeast
Typographers/Meriden, Connecticut
Designed by Thomas James Aaron
Illustrations by Dolli Tingle